This
Bible Story Time
book belongs to

ANDREW TAYLOR

604 - 8074588

For Lucy – E.C.

Text by Sophie Piper
Illustrations copyright © 2005 Estelle Corke
This edition copyright © 2005 Lion Hudson

The moral rights of the author and illustrator
have been asserted

A Lion Children's Book
an imprint of
Lion Hudson plc
Wilkinson House, Jordan Hill Road,
Oxford OX2 8DR, England
www.lionhudson.com
UK ISBN 978 0 7459 4862 1
US ISBN 978 0 8254 7813 0

First edition 2005
3 5 7 9 10 8 6 4 2

A catalogue record for this book is available
from the British Library

Typeset in 20/25 Baskerville MT Schlbk
Printed and bound in China

Distributed by:
UK: Marston Book Services Ltd, PO Box 269, Abingdon, Oxon OX14 4YN
USA: Trafalgar Square Publishing, 814 N Franklin Street, Chicago, IL 60610
USA Christian Market: Kregel Publications, PO Box 2607, Grand Rapids, Michigan 49501

BIBLE STORY TIME

Noah and the Flood

Sophie Piper ✳ Estelle Corke

LI❀N
CHILDREN'S

Long ago, there lived a man named Noah. He and his wife had three sons. The three sons each had a wife.

'Perhaps I'll have grandchildren soon,' said Noah to himself.

He began to dream of happy times ahead.

As Noah sat dreaming, he heard
a voice.

'I am unhappy,' said the voice.
'I made a good world, but people
nowadays do very bad things.'

'Who's that speaking?' said Noah
to himself. 'The one who made the
world, hmm?

'Oh! It must be God!'

'I want to begin the world again,'
said God to Noah. 'I want you to
help me.'

Noah listened carefully to
everything God said.

Then Noah went to talk to the family. 'God wants us to build a boat,' he said. 'A very big boat. God has given me instructions and lots of measurements.

'Now to begin, we must fetch some good strong wood…'

The work began. Together they built a boat with three decks and a door. They put waterproof tar on the outside.

'Now we must fetch the animals,'
said Noah. 'A mother and a father
of every kind.'

What a job it was! What a noisy
job!

'We need food too,' said Noah.
'Food for us and food for the
animals.'

growl

roa[

squeak

tweet

tweet

13

In the end, the work was done.
Everyone and everything were
safely on board.

God shut the door.

The rain started to fall. Pitter-
patter, pitter-patter. Splish-splash.

Soon the rain was tumbling down.
Splosh-splosh-splosh-splosh-splosh-splosh-splosh.

It rained and rained and rained.
And rained.
The flood began to rise. Up and
up and up. And up.

'Look,' said Noah's wife, 'the whole world is like one big sea.'

'And there's only us left,' said Noah.

He looked down at the grey water.

He looked up at the grey sky.

'I hope God hasn't forgotten us,' said Noah.

God had not forgotten. God sent
a wind that blew and blew.
  Whoo-ooh, whoo-ooh, whoo-ooh.
  Trickle by trickle, the flood began
to go down until one day…
  BUMP.
  'We've landed,' announced
Noah. 'Somewhere.'

Not long after, they
saw they were on
a mountaintop.
Noah sent a raven
out from the boat.
It flapped and flapped
and flew away.

'I'll try again,' said Noah. He sent
a dove out from the boat. The first
time it went, it flew out and flew
back. The second time it went, the
dove came back with an olive leaf.

Everyone on the ark cheered.

'The flood is over,' said God. 'Let the animals go. Tell them all to have families. I want them to fill the world again.'

Out they went. What a noise!

'Now it's time for you to go,' said God to Noah. 'You and your family must make new homes for yourselves. You must fill the world with people again.'

Out in the bright, clean world, Noah and his family had a big party.

'Look,' said God. 'I have put a rainbow in the sky. It is the sign of my promise. I will never flood the world again.'

Noah smiled. Now he knew that for ever and ever there would be summer and winter.

For ever and ever there would be a time to sow seeds and a time to harvest crops.

God's world would be a home for
his grandchildren, and his great
grandchildren... for everyone.